Let Them Play

A Parenting and Coaching Guide to Youth Sports

ERIC BYRNES

Let Them Play

A Parenting and Coaching Guide to Youth Sports

Eric Byrnes

ISBN: 979-8-35093-104-4

Dedication

This is dedicated to all of the coaches in my life whose influence has helped create the core fabric for this book. Specifically, I want to express my gratitude to the two greatest coaches I've ever had in my life, Mom and Dad.

Thank you for a lifetime of experiences that have helped our family accumulate the education that has shaped the moral compass and codes of conduct for our family as well as the entire *Let Them Play* organization.

About the Author

Eric Byrnes is a former eleven-year MLB player, Emmy award-winning broadcaster, Savannah Bananas manager, founder of the *Let Them Play* Foundation, director/coach for the *Let Them Play* nationally ranked travel ball organization and speed golf Guinness Book of World Records holder for playing 420 holes of golf while running 106 miles in twenty-four hours. Eric and his wife, Tarah, have three kids: Chloe, fourteen, Cali, thirteen, and Colton, twelve, all passionately pursuing their different sports and ways in life.

Table of Contents

Introduction

A few years ago, while playing in our very first travel ball tournament, the newly formed *Let Them Play* 10U squad (comprised solely of eight and nine-year-olds) was in the championship game against a much older and more seasoned group of players.

Clinging to a one-run lead in the middle of the game, the other team had runners at first and third with two outs . . . Our catcher called time out and walked to the mound while instructing the entire team to meet on the bump.

This is the point when Troy Glaus, John Gall, and Josh Whitesell (the three other coaches who all happened to have played in the big leagues at some point) asked if I was going to go out there to instruct the boys on what to do if the runner from first attempted to steal second.

I immediately, and instinctually, took two steps toward the field and then for whatever reason, stopped myself . . .

"Nah, they got this!"

Troy, Gall, and Whitesell all looked at me as if I was nuts and then Glaus said . . . "Well . . . This ought to be entertaining."

The boys dispersed with shit-eating grins on their faces, hustled back to their positions and it was on.

Our pitcher had a very quick slide step to home; our catcher received it beautifully and then quickly fired the ball to second base ... That's where our shortstop cut in front of the bag, caught the ball and then threw an absolute dart to home plate.

The planning of the game by the boys and the execution could not have gone much better.

To say, I was proud would have been a massive understatement, but there were a couple of minor problems ...

1. The runners from both first and third never stole.

2. The ball trickled off our catcher's glove, allowing the runner from third, who was not going, to come in to score.

Sure, the run tied the game, but the autonomy granted to the kids to let them call that game on their own was a defining moment for how this team and organization was and is going to be run.

When the boys got back to the dugout, we commended them for the play call, corrected them on the nearly impeccable, yet unnecessary, execution, and ultimately, we all had a pretty good laugh.

As the game progressed, you could visually see the freedom and fearlessness of our kids continue to become bolder while the pressure and tension continued to rise in the other dugout.

Three-zero monster hacks, relentlessly ripping bags, our right fielder laying out for a Superman catch and another little grom stealing home on the throwback to the pitcher helped solidify the first-ever LTP Championship and set the standard for how *Let Them Play* was going to attack the game.

When we let the kids play by allowing them to make decisions on their own as opposed to holding their hand and dictating every move, the kids' baseball IQ as well as their confidence will exponentially escalate at rapid rates.

As a parent or coach, releasing the reins can sound great in theory, but hard to put into practice. This book delves into the when, what, and how to *Let Them Play*!

What Is *Let Them Play?*

The mission of *Let Them Play* is very simple: Do everything in our power as coaches and parents to ensure we get the most out of players and teams while providing a free, fearless and fun environment predicated on work.

Here we reveal a revolutionary and eternally evolving playing, coaching, and parenting philosophy developed through years of experience across many fields of life.

This *"Let Them Play"* philosophical approach has helped the Savannah Bananas to become a household name while at the same time leading the *Let Them Play* travel ball organization to national prominence . . .

The cornerstone of Let Them Play is exactly as it sounds. We, as parents and coaches, need to focus on developing the athletes so that they are empowered to own their path, to let them play. Through trial, failure, success, hard work, and relentlessness, our kids and athletes will be prepared for the road ahead.

Understanding Our Role

In order to understand coaching and parenting, we must first understand the different phases of development our kids will go through in their life and athletic journey. Through my experience as a player, parent, and coach, I've concluded that there are three different periods in a young athlete's development that unquestionably require three very different parenting and coaching strategies and actions.

The first is what we will refer to as "the planting seed" years, ages one through six.

The second phase of the athlete's development is "the formative years," ages seven to twelve.

The third and final period of development and influence we will have on that maturation process is what we will refer to as "the guiding years," ages thirteen and beyond.

Our goal is to produce athletes who know and love their sport. Athletes that have confidence in their training and instincts because they have been battle tested and perfected. Athletes and children who are prepared and practiced at owning their path.

As the great stoic philosopher Epictetus once said . . .

"That is what I trained for."

Sports are an incredible outlet for young go-hards to display their emotions while developing not only as athletes but most importantly as human beings. The takeaway from these on-field experiences is so far beyond the trophy, but it's up to us to help bring them to light. Being a coach or parent to an athlete, you are entrusted to be the gatekeeper and illuminator to these lessons. Ultimately, our ability to recognize and appropriately convey these teachings is what will get our kids to value them. Good luck :)

Planting Seeds

Our job as a parent at the ages from one to six years old is simply to introduce our kids to all sorts of various sports and to do everything in our power to make it a pleasurable experience that the kids are eager to repeat. This stage is not about competition; it is about exposing young athletes to the joy of sport, and all the sports that may call to them. It is about developing their desire to play.

When I think back to my vague memories of sports in my early life, I remember these things . . .

1. Whacking and chucking tennis balls with my sister and parents.

2. Ripping down a ski mountain between my dad's legs.

3. Going to the karate studio to play while my dad would teach.

4. Playing tackle football with my best friend in his front yard.

5. Playing baseball with my neighbor.

6. Scoring a boatload of goals for the "Orange Crush" playing soccer for the first time.

7. Firing a basketball at some sort of circular metal thing.

My parents were planting seeds for trees which they knew very well I may never sit under, but they continued to plant them anyway.

The greatest lesson I learned in these years was an immense love for playing sports and even more importantly, a love for being active.

When it came time for my wife Tarah and me to introduce our kids to the world, we both thought about what we loved as kids and then we were aggressive about doing everything in our power to provide similar experiences.

Obviously, we all come from different backgrounds and available resources, but here are a few of the sports that we strategically tried to "plant the seed" for the sole purpose of providing an awesome base for whatever our kids inevitably decided that they loved and wanted to pursue.

I want to emphasize, that we did not introduce these sports to our kids at this age with the intention of turning them into child prodigies with professional sports aspirations. It was simply about exposing them to various sports and then figuring out what brought the most amount of joy to their lives.

> **Outside**-I know, it is not a sport, but it's a great place to start. Go outside, chase butterflies, play

in the grass, jump hopscotch, hike around, get in the water, climb trees. This is where kids start to learn how to move their bodies, and how much better they feel afterward, and it is very importantly, self-directed. Throw them in the backyard and lock the door ...

Skiing-As soon as the kids could walk, they were on skis. Living in Lake Tahoe we didn't have much of a choice. It even meant that Tarah had to learn :)

Running-We tried to teach the kids about the physical and mental rewards of running very early on. It's still a rule in our house that there are zero electronics until a mile is complete.

Surfing-As soon as they could swim, we got them on a board and in the ocean. Letting kids experience and understand the power of the ocean at an early age has a tremendous impact and teaches them the extreme importance of always respecting Mother Nature.

Skateboarding-Around the block on the boards with the kids became one of our favorite pastimes. Core strength, situational awareness, and balance are all on full display and have tremendous benefits.

Karate-A must for all kids as soon as they are old enough and the instructor is willing to take them. Age five or six typically is a good starting point.

This is often the first introduction to real discipline outside of the house. The self-discipline, self-defense, body awareness, and control that are learned are all invaluable tools for life.

Gymnastics-Another must sport in my opinion that provides an all-around athletic base for all other sports. It also is usually one of the first sports kids can participate in. A key place to develop vestibular sense or as we call it, court awareness, knowing where one's body is in space and how it is moving.

Tennis-A racket, a ball, and a wall, simple introduction to hand-eye coordination at its finest.

Front yard baseball-I fired Tennis Ball (TB) Cheddar Cheese to the kids at an early age and to this point they still haven't seen a faster pitcher :) Tee-ball is cool, TB Cheddar Cheese is better. Plus, it takes some solid nerve to stand in against it. Train hard to play easy.

Football-Just an object to throw and something to tackle. Kids like throwing things and hitting things. Body awareness benefits are huge.

Soccer-An easy and fantastic introduction to team sports, any sport that makes exercise fun at this age is a great option. Footwork and teamwork benefits will last way beyond the soccer field.

Organized sports before age six:

Because he could hit the ball really well for his age, when Colton was three, Tarah tried to put him in Tee-ball . . . bad idea.

Colton was playing some variation of shortstop and every time the ball was hit, he would run and get it. The issue was that if the ball was hit to second, third, or the outfield, he would get those, too!

Eventually, the coach drew a circle at shortstop and told Colton he had to stay in the circle. That's the exact time Colton walked off the field, handed me his glove, and said, "I don't want to play baseball anymore, Daddy."

He quit for three years.

The coach's intentions were fine, and I imagine he drew the circle so the other kids would not have to worry about Colton running over to get the ball. That said, we learned that day that nobody was going to keep Colton, aka Biscuit, in a box.

Over the next three years, we would play catch all the time while slowly introducing him to the infamous TB Cheddar Cheese game.

The goal at this age is to teach the kid to love the sport and develop the habit of activity. Kids can play organized sports, as long as the emphasis is on fun and development, not competition and rules.

Note to all coaches and parents: The development of throwing a ball and hitting a ball happens at a pretty rapid rate. Catching a baseball, on the other hand, will be the last of the beautiful baseball trifecta to master for the young go-hard.

When Colton was four, we took him to the Super Bowl in Santa Clara and we brought our gloves and baseball so we could play catch during the pre-game tailgate. At this point, we were playing catch nearly every day, and upon his relentless requests, I had just recently introduced the hard baseball as opposed to the soft ones we had been using for a number of years. He loved the fact that he finally got to throw a real baseball!

I tossed him a few to get comfortable then slowly began to pick up the velocity. He was swiping the balls out of the air like he was Rickey Henderson in his prime and even picked a few of my errant throws.

I remember turning toward the stadium in the background and thinking how cool it was that Biscuit's first day of real catch with a real baseball was happening at the Super Bowl. I couldn't help, but get a bit nostalgic thinking of the games of catch that I had with my dad out in front of Candlestick Park before a 49ers or Giants game.

I then fired Colton one last ball before we headed into the stadium.

Whack!

The ball hit him square in the nose and blood began to profusely squirt everywhere.

Apparently, we jumped to the hardball just a bit too soon!

Catching a ball is difficult for kids to learn mainly because they catch with their non-dominant hand. There are so many ways to position the body and hand when it comes to properly catching a baseball. For instance, forehand, backhand, underhand, and overhead are all ways to catch a baseball and most catches actually happen to be some variation or combination of the four.

Ultimately, it's up to you, but my recommendation would be to leave the hardball at home until the kids are at least six and extremely comfortable catching a ball in all directions. Using a softer baseball or even a tennis ball is much better at a young age anyway because you can throw them way harder without any fear of an emergency room visit.

Letting Go

Arm strength with Biscuit was never an issue, but I was a bit concerned about his throwing mechanics. They seemed a bit short-armed to me who just so happens to be a long-armed throwing outfielder.

In the "planting seed" years, I consistently did everything I could to get him to lengthen his throwing motion, but he would always revert back to what was natural to him. Finally, when he was nine and throwing absolute gas on the mound as well as throwing runners out from behind the dish, I realized, how grateful I was that he never listened to me.

This was one of the very first times that I realized that in order to get the best out of my kid, or any other kid for that matter, we oftentimes need to step back, stop coaching and let their natural order take over.

Bottomline: The planting seed years should be spent doing exactly that . . . Planting seeds. What inevitably grows from the seeds we plant is not always up to us and oftentimes, a flower we never expected will blossom.

The Formative Years

These are the years, ages seven to twelve, when each day can feel like a miracle of gargantuan progress or like our kids are running backward on a treadmill. We share in the ecstasy of progress and oftentimes crumble way harder than the kids do in their defeat.

Progress and success are not linear, it's a roller coaster ride that involves getting better or worse each day. Whether or not we like it, all of us are only as good as our next performance.

Sure, this may sound a bit harsh when we are talking about seven to twelve-year-old kids, but we are not here to prepare the road for the child; we are here to prepare the child for the road.

Although ages from seven to twelve may seem a bit young, it is our job as parents, coaches, and mentors to hold kids accountable for their attitude, effort, preparation, and performance. From there, it is also our job to give them the tools to get better while making sure the overall experience is both enjoyable and fun.

Sound easy?

It's not, but rest assured, it is very doable.

Here's how . . .

Pat them on the back and kick them in the ass.

For years, we have debated whether to pat a kid on the back or kick him in the ass (not actually, but metaphorically). The reality is that no matter who that kid is, we must do both.

Of course, we as human beings are all different and obviously kids are all different, but no matter who we are, we all need positive reinforcement and we all need correction.

When we skew too far in one direction, we ruin the kid.

For instance, Little Johnny is having a tough time at the plate. He struck out his last three plate appearances, swung at a ball in the dirt, and two other pitches that were over his head. He comes back to the dugout looking dejected and gives us that blank stare. We essentially have three ways to deal with Little Johnny . . .

1. Pat-on-the-back approach-"Hey, Little Johnny, you look good, you are just missing those pitches . . . Go get 'em next time!"

   Little Johnny's thoughts-"*Do you think I am stupid? I don't look good, I wasn't even close to those pitches and why are you feeding me this bullshit?*"

2. Kick-in-the-ass approach-"Hey, Little Johnny, what exactly are you swinging at? You couldn't hit those

pitches with a ten-foot oar and as a matter of fact, I'm not sure if you could hit water if you fell out of a boat."

Little Johnny's thoughts–"*I suck, I want to go home.*"

3. Pat-on-the back **and** kick-in-the-ass approach–"Hey, Little Johnny, I know you are frustrated right now but you aren't that far off. Your swing is actually looking pretty good, but as you know, the number one rule to hitting is we have to get a good ball to hit. Not even Mike Trout could have hit those pitches you swung at.

   Next time up, do me a favor . . . The only thing I want you to do is to see the ball immediately out of the pitcher's hand. From there, it's just a matter of making sure it's a good pitch to hit and trust your swing. That's it!"

   Little Johnny's thoughts–"Coach is right, my swing is legit. All I have to do is swing at strikes and it's on! Okay . . . Just see the ball out of the hand . . . I can't wait for my next at bat!"

   The "pat-on-the-back and kick-in-the-ass" approach provided Johnny with specific and accurate praise while offering him direction toward reaching his ultimate goal through constructive insight.

   Delivery, honesty, and simplicity are keys to this approach.

On the flip side, now let's imagine that Little Johnny is crushing it! He's three for his last three with a beautiful line drive single, an opposite gap double, and an absolute nuke! He comes back to the dugout and all his teammates are in awe and praising him for his success. Little Johnny looks at us for approval and we once again have three ways we can deal with it . . .

1. Pat-on-the-back approach-"Dude, you are amazing! Even though you are only twelve, I have no idea how you haven't received any college scholarship offers yet? First round or bust, Little Johnny. Next stop, the show!"

   Little Johnny's thoughts-"*I am the next Aaron Judge, but better. Bryce Harper doesn't have anything on me. This game is too easy. I should be playing at a higher level.*"

2. Kick-in-the-ass approach-"You got lucky. All three pitchers you just hit sucked. I'd like to see you do it against real competition in a game that actually meant something."

   Little Johnny's thoughts-"*Nothing is ever good enough . . . It doesn't matter what I do, coach still thinks I suck. I am doing well and this isn't even fun.*"

3. Pat-on-the-back **and** kick-in-the-ass approach- "Little Johnny, stay right there."

   Little Johnny's thoughts-"*Okay.*"

   The "pat-on-the-back and kick-in-the-ass" approach in this situation provides Johnny with the positive reinforcement he needs while reminding him to continue to work. He can be proud of his success without letting it stop his progress.

It's amazing how influential a coach's or parents' words can be within the formative seven to twelve years. Words still matter for kids aged between one and six as well as thirteen and beyond, but when kids are younger, they are very forgetful and incredibly resilient. When they are older, they often don't listen to us anyway. Yet, our words within these very impressionable, formative years are as impactful as they will ever be. They literally have the ability to make, or break a kid's psyche and career.

We must be sure to correct any and all mistakes, but we must also be sure to never condemn.

Ultimately, it's pretty simple . . . Choose words wisely.

During "the formative years," let's do our best to form the athletes into confident yet humble, hardworking, appreciative little savages who understand the value of learning through success and failure, capable of hearing and implementing both constructive and praise-filled feedback.

Bottomline: Fun wins and during the formative years, we will be creating memories that will last a lifetime; let's make sure they are fun ones that will inspire the kids to just keep playing!

The Guiding Years

As much as we like to believe, we are still forming the child, in fact, the child at this point may actually be forming us for what's to come.

Ah, f*ck . . . Now what?

Just be there.

Be there to guide the kid who is on the precipice of adulthood. They are dealing with unimaginable hormones and mood swings so don't take any sort of snaps personally; they are still trying to find themselves in their new body and developing mind. Work hard to meet angst with calm and anger with patience. We should always hold them accountable to be good person, but empathy and grace in these years is critical.

Preparation and Approach-At this age, the biggest impact we can have is by teaching them how to properly prepare while maintaining a consistent approach to the game and life. Teach them about the value of a routine and then help them create one that works within the confines of their schedule.

Ultimately, whether or not your child or star player "makes it," however you want to define that term, isn't up to us. It is solely up to them and their obsession to be great.

Make no mistake about this very critical fact . . .

If you want to be great, you have to be obsessed.

Whether or not a kid becomes obsessed is completely outside of our control. Sure, we can lead the horse to water and we might even be able to force that horse to take a few sips, but in order for the horse to take down the entire trough, that horse must be obsessed.

You name the greatest athletes of all time and the number one trait every single one of them had was an obsession to be great.

> Michael Jordan-Obsessed
>
> Lance Armstrong-Obsessed
>
> Mikaela Shiffrin-Obsessed
>
> Barry Bonds-Obsessed
>
> Tom Brady-Obsessed
>
> Tony Gwynn-Obsessed
>
> Serena Williams-Obsessed
>
> Tiger Woods-Obsessed

This list goes on and on. Many of these same people had their obsession eventually work against them. The same obsession that made them the best at their craft inevitably backfired and contributed heavily to their demise.

With obsession often comes selfishness and a win-at-all-cost attitude which can often blur the lines of right and wrong.

If we are fortunate to parent and/or coach an "obsessed" athlete, it's imperative to continue to guide the obsession in the right direction. Obsess the process, not the outcome. The neglect of elements of the process such as balance, joy, sleep, and overall long-term health are what so often contribute to an unhealthy obsession. Obsess work ethic, process, progress, effort, attitude, and a little bit of grace. Let the kids' obsession work for them and not against them.

For instance, there was no question that from the time I was thirteen years old until I walked away from the game at thirty-four, I was obsessed.

During my high school football season, I would wake up and hit a hundred baseballs before school and then bang out a hundred more under makeshift lighting in the darkness after football practice. Everything I did, everything I read, everything I watched, every conversation I had was done under the pretense of "How will this make me a better baseball player?"

Being on the football team made me a better baseball player, and I knew it. Developing general athleticism and footwork while playing other sports was vital in my overall development as an athlete.

The good thing for me was that I poured my obsession into my work and whenever I faced any sort of failure, disappointment, or adversity, the solution was simple: work harder, work longer, work smarter.

Right or wrong, how we react to failure is how people will ultimately judge our character. When we react with excuses and idleness by taking our ball and going home, we will be perceived as quitters, incapable of handling adversity. Yet, when we respond with accountability and work, we will be viewed as a great teammate who has a burning desire to get better.

Obsession can be a great thing, but it must be controlled and it's imperative we teach kids how to keep the proper perspective of long-term growth vs. short-term rewards when dealing with losses and other perceived failures. There is no shortcut to the top, and hard work is the only way to get there.

Kids watch how coaches and parents react to adversity and then more often than not, they mirror our behavior. When we make excuses, they make excuses. When we are over-emotional, they are over-emotional. When we are accountable, they are accountable. When we maintain proper perspective, they typically will maintain proper perspective.

The 'Baseball is Life' mantra that dominated the 90s and early 2000s is a fun saying, but even with the obsession, it's bullshit.

Baseball is a game and it consumes the lives of the obsessed, but by no means is baseball life. Life is defined by our relationships with God, family, and friends. Life is ultimately measured by the knowledge accumulated through our experiences and then our ability to pass on that knowledge to the next generation of hard chargers. Life is making sure we do everything in our power to leave people and things better than we found them. Life is learning. Life is loving. Life is giving. Life is listening. Life is mentoring. Life is teaching. Life is coaching. Life is dreaming. Life is hoping. Life is believing. Life is experiencing. Life is a lot of f*cking things, but baseball, or any other sport, is not one of them.

Bottomline: When dealing with young adults in the thirteen and above "guiding years," let's make sure we do just that . . . Guide.

Guide the kid to establish a relentless work ethic.

Guide the kid to establish a routine.

Guide the kid to establish a consistent approach.

Guide the kid to establish a positive mindset.

Guide the kid to all of the necessary tools that will help them build and maintain their establishments.

Then . . . Just be there.

Cornerstones

We have talked about the stages of our athletes and when we are focused on certain goals. But what are the cornerstones of inspiring, developing, and guiding a confident, self-motivated athlete and child? Our *Let Them Play* philosophy focuses on four concepts to motivate and infuse our decisions.

Passion, Energy, and Effort

It is the heartbeat of how we approach sports, and ultimately, all the things we pursue. It is even the official "handshake" of our baseball teams.

Process over Product

Is what we are doing focused on making us better, not just getting a "best result?" Winning, or whatever determinant of success we use, should be a by-product of the process, not the goal.

Attitude and Effort

Attitude and effort are simply the only two things always under our control.

Something Bigger

Sports is a tremendous arena for learning and developing imperative life skills like teamwork, discipline, tenacity, and focus. Remembering there is something bigger happening can power anyone through the bumps.

Passion, Energy, Effort

Passion, Energy and Effort are the guiding principles of the *Let Them Play* organization and are applicable to all sports and all arenas of life. The question becomes what exactly are these principles and how do we apply them at the three different stages of the planting seed, formative and guiding years?

First off, let's quickly define the three.

> Passion: An immense commitment and will to do whatever it takes to complete the task at hand.

> Energy: Energy is everything; without it we are dead. When we are juicefull, we are useful, when we are juiceless, we are f*ing useless.

> Effort: One of the very few things that we can control and be consistent with throughout our entire careers and life.

One-six: Demonstrate excitement for play and honor any and all efforts to try something new.

Seven-twelve: Instill all three in everything that the kids do. Put passion into the process of getting better. Put energy into the relentless process of getting better. Put effort into doing the things that they don't necessarily always want to do.

Thirteen and beyond: Get specific. Passion, energy, and effort should be reflected in specific goals and actions.

Most importantly, we must let our passion as a parent and coach be the guiding light showing the kids how to properly compete with an immense intensity while always maintaining our own dignity and ultimate respect for the competition and officials involved. We must let our energy radiate positivity and love for the sport and all of the countless hours of work that is so diligently demanded. Last, but certainly not least, we must let our effort reflect our commitment to both excellence and growth.

Process over Product

Our baseball teams use the construct of "Battle For Barrels" to make sure we are rewarding the process over the product. A barrel is any ball that is classified as "hard hit" and is immediately awarded with a Slim Jim or some form of candy regardless of the outcome it produced.

Eventually, repetition of the proper process will produce the results we are looking for but the only way to get there is to be over-consumed with the specific activities and actions that will lead us there.

Here are a few process-oriented things we can focus on and reward when we see them done correctly.

1. Work Ethic-Defined by attitude and effort as well as the willingness to listen, learn, and work.

2. Routines-Pre-game routine-On-deck routine-Pitching routine-Pre-pitch routine for fielders-Routines are essential.

3. Approach-Swinging at strikes-Taking balls-Attacking zone for a pitcher-Being in the proper position for fielders.

4. Execution-Barrels for hitters-Soft contact or swings and misses for pitchers-Fielders making plays regardless if an out is recorded.

5. Hustle-Doesn't take any skill to hustle and it should be celebrated at all times.

Goal Setting

When setting goals as a coach, a parent, or an athlete, it is important to set both process and product or result-oriented goals that we write down and consistently revisit and adjust accordingly.

Process goals should be prioritized and seen as the ultimate path to the product goals.

In Skiing, high-level athletes train 300 days a year and compete in their craft for the entire season in less than thirty cumulative minutes. World-class sprinter Usain Bolt once famously said, "I trained four years to run nine seconds, and people give up when they don't see results in two months."

It's imperative that these athletes have process goals in order to progress so they don't ever have to deal with those feelings of giving up.

Process Goals: Goals that commit a certain amount of work and time with controllable results specifically dedicated to improving your craft.

Here are three examples of process goals for a baseball or softball player.

1. Offensive/Defensive Drills-Fielding and cage work driven by established and ever-evolving routines.

2. Journaling-After-games or after-training sessions are both great times to document our observations and reflect upon what went right, what went wrong, and the adjustments we could make moving forward.

3. Cross Training-We must dedicate a certain amount of time to strength training as well as participation in dynamic training and speed work.

All of these are process goals that can be easily set, pursued, and accomplished which then allows us to set realistic production goals.

Production Goals: Various goals are typically tied directly to results.

Here are three examples of production goals for a baseball or softball player.

1. Three points-We are often obsessed with getting hits but a walk, sacrifice, run scored, RBI, or great play in the field is just as important in helping us win games. Think of each one as a point and when we can consistently tally up at least three points a day, our contribution to the team will be both consistent and significant. By the way, a double counts as two points, a triple-three and a homer four.

2. Barrel Barrage-Barrels are part of the process that inevitably produce results so this one may be viewed by some as a "process goal" but ultimately barrels aren't always controllable so we will put it under the "production goal" category. Assuming we get four at-bats, the goal of two hard-hit balls per game or a fifty percent barrel rate would be fantastic and a lofty goal to shoot for.

3. Walks > Strikeouts-Loved this one when I played because it would promote both patience in waiting for a ball to drive while also incentivizing battling to put the ball in play with two strikes.

One-six: There shouldn't be "products" at this age . . . We are focused on the process, the love of play, and the habit of being active.

Seven-twelve: Winning is fun, but for it to be a long-term experience, kids need to focus on what gets them there, not just being there. Help them along by focusing on process, and rewarding advances and obtainment of process goals.

Thirteen and beyond: By now, process should be an integral part of their approach. Help your athlete and child fine-tune these goals for their sport, and enjoy the delight they experience when hard work starts to pay off.

Attitude and Effort

As coaches and parents, our attitude and our efforts are a direct reflection of who we are and who we aspire to be. Attitude and effort are the two things that we, and the kids, have the ability to control in this very volatile and uncontrollable world. The earlier we are able to hammer that home, the better chance the kids will have for properly dealing with inevitable adverse situations such as rough weather, a tough pitcher, or a shitty umpire.

So long as the kids have the right attitude and the right effort, every other controllable element, including preparation and approach, should properly fall into place.

We are introducing the incredible value of work ethic, preparation, and hustle while making sure the kids understand that the only thing they will ever get out of anything is what they put in.

When the game is no longer fun, we lose the kids and we fail as parents and coaches. Ultimately, whether the kid plays a day past twelve years old is not up to us, it's one hundred percent up to the kid; so let's do our best to make sure they love their sport enough to keep playing.

One-six: Fun is the name of this game! As coaches and parents, if our focus stays on the fun part at this age, so will theirs. Good attitudes and real efforts should be the crux of 'success' at this age and celebrated beyond the product of these behaviors.

Seven-twelve: Feelings get "big" at this age and reminding our kids and athletes to be good humans first and foremost will help focus a productive attitude and inspire solid effort. Getting this piece straight will definitely determine the enjoyment and experience.

Thirteen and beyond: Our athletes need to know that people are watching. Remind them to be contributors, positive, and accepting of constructive advice. If it's scouts, coaches, future employers, or future in-laws, don't behave in a way that will burn bridges and leave a bad taste. More and more, high level coaches are focusing on the attitude and the coachability of their prospects.

Something Bigger

If the purpose isn't to become an elite athlete, then why work so hard and invest so much? Because the skills, lessons, and characteristics that are learned and honed through sports are difference-makers in the "game" of life.

Being a part of a team is powerful. There is a proverb that says "To go far, go together." But it isn't always easy to be a teammate. Practicing how to put a team first over your own ambitions, learning how to support those that need it, and accepting there will be times when you carry the load and when you are the one that gets picked up. These are all things that will make someone a better person, not just a better athlete.

Understanding that work is the path to results is well-versed in sports. This will never handicap someone while they pursue their education, career, or anything else outside of sports.

We learn in sports that if you aren't failing, you aren't pushing the line. And that if you do "fail," you pick yourself up, apply the lesson, listen to the advice, and try again. Experiencing winning and losing cannot be taught. It must be done. And with those experiences comes the practice to make it work for you, to view it with a positive, balanced mindset, and the joy of achieving the goal in spite of setback.

The skills a child learns and practices in any sport will support and enable all of their pursuits. There is no substitute for actually experiencing teamwork, self-discipline, failure, success, and tenacity. As they go through these elements in their development, they gain confidence to use them throughout their life. A loss can't knock them down because they have already experienced that is just a part of something bigger.

One-six: Early sports development will give young kids more tools to succeed in early education. Remind them that being a part of a unit is powerful, as it's a naturally self-centered time in their development.

Seven-twelve: Experiencing success and failure in sports will empower this age to handle it with confidence as they move forward and go through educational and social growth. It takes a lot of bricks to make a building, and that is what they are doing.

Thirteen and beyond: Now we can talk about how what they are doing at this stage will absolutely shape their future. Sports and their lessons, especially how you respond to them, will be a huge part of higher education, careers, and relationships. Encourage your athletes to invest in themselves.

The Rules

There are three rules in our family and for our LTP teams.

No Whiners

Be Kind

Go Hard

Simple, but clear, if our kids are adhering to these rules, they are getting the job done right.

The lessons of sports easily translate to lessons in life and we should never shy away from highlighting this crossover. Our words unquestionably are the precursor to our actions but before we get into the *Let Them Play* creed and codes of conduct, please understand that they are only as effective as our ability to adhere to them.

Parents, coaches, and players alike, all must hold themselves accountable to both the creed and the codes. The upcoming teachings are much bigger than sports and have the potential to positively impact every one of us for the rest of our lives but as my dad used to religiously remind me . . .

"We must let our actions reflect our commitment."

Creed and Codes
of Conduct

Through the first three years of *Let Them Play's* existence, we had nearly a hundred kids play for our one team across three different age groups.

As the kids and awesome experiences continued to pile up, we realized that in order to have the maximum impact, we had no choice but to expand. Our goal was to create an organization based on playing and teaching the game the right way; a way that focused on development, process, accountability, and empowered athletes. We also wanted to build something that would have the potential to outlive all of us.

So, in the fall of 2022, our *Let Them Play* squad officially expanded and we added several new coaches and age groups. Most of the coaches I had either played with or coached with before and they were well aware of the way *Let Them Play* went about playing and coaching the game.

That said, it was inevitable that each team was going to have several new players and coaches who have never been a part of LTP, so to uphold the spirit and integrity of the organization, we created a *Let Them Play* Creed as well as twenty-two playing, coaching, and parenting codes of conduct we fully expect everyone within the LTP organization to adhere to.

Like anything in life, we fully understand that the below creed as well as the codes of conduct are subject to change at any point if we feel that we could add or subtract something that would add value to the organization.

Though this is clearly directed toward baseball, the spirit of the creed and the codes goes well beyond. So, if you are reading this as a pickleball player, you can re-adjust the information about stealing bases and apply it to your game with the relentlessness and intensity that we talk about

On that note, get the highlighter out and enjoy as we humbly and proudly publicly present the *Let Them Play* creed and playing, coaching, and parenting codes of conduct.

Let Them Play Creed

I want to preface this Creed by saying I have the utmost respect for our armed forces members (past and present.) Using the Seal Ethos as the foundation for our Creed is not in any way comparing what goes on a battlefield as being even remotely similar to what happens on a ball field. Yet, a surefire way to become the best is to learn from the best, and in this case, the Navy Seals have proven over the years to be one of the greatest teams in any industry or any sport ever assembled.

Let Them Play Creed–(Based on Navy Seal Ethos)

In times of challenging practices or games, there is a special breed of ballplayers ready to step up in any and all situations . . . A common baller with an uncommon desire to succeed . . . Forged by adversity, they stand alongside some of the very best, most well prepared go-hard savages in this nation, ready to do whatever it takes to help their team win.

I am that dude.

Let Them Play is a symbol of honor and heritage . . . Bestowed upon me by the players and coaches who have gone before; it embodies the trust of the team I have sworn to represent. By wearing a *Let Them Play* uniform, I accept the responsibility of my opportunity and dedicate myself to freely and fearlessly playing this great game.

With great freedoms come great responsibilities . . . I will be responsible for my freedoms and grateful for every opportunity that comes my way.

Success is not owned, it's leased and rent is due every single day ... I will pay the rent.

We are only as good as our next performance ...

Our work is never finished ...

Tomorrow is reserved for the labor of the lazy ... I will work now.

Pressure is a privilege ...

I will earn that privilege.

My loyalty to the organization and team is beyond reproach. I humbly serve as a guardian to all my teammates and I am willing and ready to pick up those who may be unable to pick up themselves in that moment.

I do not advertise the nature of my work nor seek recognition for my actions. I voluntarily accept whatever position I am asked to play and whatever spot in the order I am assigned to hit, placing the welfare of the team before my own.

I will honor the game.

I will respect my coaches.

I will respect my teammates.

I will respect the umpires.

I will respect my opponent but fear no one.

There is no pitcher, batter, or fielder too difficult ...

We want the best, we need the best, and we are the best.

Iron sharpens iron.

I am iron.

I will never quit. I will persevere and thrive on adversity. My team expects me to be physically harder and mentally stronger than our opponent.

When it's too tough for them, it's just right for us.

If knocked down, I will get back up, every time . . .

I will draw on my training as well as my past successes to give me the strength to battle, no matter the situation or circumstance.

We are never out of the fight.

The ability to control my emotions and actions, regardless of circumstance, sets me apart from others . . .

Uncompromising passion, energy, and effort is my standard. My character, attitude, and hustle are steadfast.

My preparation reflects my commitment.

We expect to lead and be led . . . In the absence of orders, I will take charge, lead my teammates, and execute the play . . . I lead by example in all situations.

We demand discipline . . . We expect innovation . . . The success of the team depends on my ability to adapt, adjust, and overcome . . . My skills must be trained . . . My training is never complete.

We train hard to play EZ. I stand ready to fully send my effort in every game, in every play; in any way . . .There simply is no other option.

My execution will be efficient, effective and in the rare case it is required, violent, but always guided by three basic rules . . .

No Whiners, Be Kind, Go Hard.

My attention to detail is superior. My situational awareness is next level. I will always keep my eye on the baseball.

We have fought to build this proud tradition and feared reputation that I am bound to uphold . . . I will uphold the character by which that tradition and reputation have been built.

In the most challenging conditions, the legacy of my team and teammates steadies my resolve and silently guides my every move.

The place is here . . . The time is now.

We will win.

We will learn.

LTP LFG.

Twenty-Two Player Codes for Conduct

These are the clear expectations we have for everyone who pulls on a *Let Them Play* uni...

1. Show Up

Well, when I was trying to figure out where to start, several things such as attitude, effort, work ethic, and preparedness were all at the forefront of core principles we wanted to see the *Let Them Play* players adhere to. That said, absolutely none of those things matter if a player does not show up to games or practices.

In my first year in professional baseball, we had a teammate who was absolutely dominant on the mound. He won Pitcher of the Year honors and was invited to the Instructional League with the other top prospects in the organization. He was seemingly going to be on the fast track to the big leagues but there was one major issue ... He didn't show up. He skipped out on instructions because he wanted to spend time with his girlfriend and then didn't show up to Spring Training because she told him she would break up with him if he left. He quit baseball and she inevitably broke up with his ass anyway.

2. No Whining

Plain and simple, whiners deny accountability and bring down team morale. Be over accountable to everything and just as legendary Buffalo Bills head coach Marv Levy reminded his team before they played in the coldest game in Bills history . . .

"When it's too tough for them, it's just right for us."

When I reached AAA, the first thing I noticed was how bitter the majority of the guys were that they weren't in the big leagues. Many of them had time in the show and believed that was where they belonged. Noticing the whiny negative energy, I distanced myself from the crowd and simply continued to relentlessly work off the field while busting my ass on it. A month and a half later, I surpassed at least two perpetual whiners who were perceived to be ahead of me on the depth chart and got called up to the big leagues. The players I passed up were incredibly talented and good dudes, but they got caught in the complaining trap and it inevitably affected their play on the field and reputation in the clubhouse.

3. Be Kind

Nobody wants to play with an asshole. We don't have to be friends with everybody on the team, but we must be cordial.

While playing with the A's, I had a huge altercation with a teammate that nearly came to blows. For the next four months of the season, we barely spoke to each other, but we were both able to set aside our differences, were respectful to one another, and cohabitated fine on the field and in the clubhouse. Eventually, we became friends again, and still would consider him a good friend today. This is an emotional game played by emotional players and we will all have our moments of rage. Yet, at the end of the day, human decency and general kindness can and will prevail.

4. Go Hard

It's a mentality expressed through actions-Don't tell me, show me . . .

I had a teammate in the big leagues who was an incredible baseball player and he played the game pretty hard most of the time. Every now and again, when things were not going his way, he would slack on the field by jogging after a ball or not running out a pop-up. Whenever we were in any sort of social setting, he would often bring up the fact, "Byrnesie, I'm just like you, we play hard!" I would politely nod my head and turn away until finally, one day, I snapped. "Look, Dude, I love you and you do play hard most of the time, but quit telling people you play hard all the time and start f*cking showing them . . . Hustle doesn't take plays off."

Team Go Hard is not something you choose on any given day . . . It's a mentality and a lifestyle that is eternal and uncompromising.

5. Full Send Everything

Don't take talent to hustle. I get that this is a bit redundant with rule number four, but I can't emphasize enough the importance of attitude and effort which is directly reflected in one's ability to not take a single play off.

Every time I popped up or rolled over a ground ball, I failed at executing my job and would take out my frustrations by running as hard as I absolutely could. Because of this, I can't tell you how many times in my career I ended up on base with a bloop double that for whatever reason was not caught or an infield single because the infielder took his sweet ass time . . . In 2006, Anibel Sanchez had a no-hitter with two outs in the ninth and I was the final hitter . . . He threw a slider down and away and I rolled over and hit a ground ball to Hanley Ramirez at shortstop . . . Hanley fielded the ball, brought both hands in the air (in a celebratory sort of move), and then fired first . . . As a base runner, I felt like I could tell if I was always safe or out because I could feel my foot hit the bag and also hear the glove pop at first base . . .

Whatever came first was the ultimate determinant . . . In this specific case, I undoubtedly felt my foot hit the bag right before I heard the pop . . . I'll never forget locking eyes with the first base umpire who also knew I had just beaten out a routine ground ball to ruin a no-no . . . The umpire hesitated for an awkward second and then eventually called me out . . . Because of the scenario and the fact the game was basically already decided, I didn't argue the call but if you go back and look up the play today, it clearly shows I beat the ball . . . Bottom line, just f*ing send it.

6. Know the Situation

Flash outs, check outfielders, check infielders . . .

It wasn't until I got to the big leagues and had Ron Washington as my third base coach that I finally put together the trifecta when I got on base. At the lower levels of baseball, many coaches do a very good job of overcomplicating shit. Oftentimes, this is done to try to prove their worth but the irony is that the higher level of baseball that you play, simplification and attention to detail becomes the predominant way of coaching the game. The player is expected to know without the coach telling them.

For instance, many third base coaches can't wait to flash through nineteen signs after every pitch, and although their intentions may be good, more than anything, all of those signs routinely divert the base runners' attention from how many outs there are, where the fielders are playing and most importantly, where the freaking ball is!

7. Never Take the Eye off the Baseball

If there is one thing I relentlessly hammered home managing the Savannah Bananas, it was to never take your eye off the baseball . . . Never ever! This not only allowed us to avoid the over-the-top hidden ball tricks but it also allowed us to take advantage of our opponent's lapses in concentration. Ripping second base when the SS and second baseman dropped their heads and turned toward the outfield or stealing third base when the third baseman was playing deep in the hole were both very common. We also had an amazing ability to '"back pick" & "hidden ball trick" Party Animals as they spent too much time dancing, talking shit, and celebrating themselves.

8. Learn to Properly Slide Headfirst

Bust out the slip-and-slide and have at it because there is no question in my mind that launching into the air like a superhero is faster. Rickey Henderson stole 1,406 bases in his career and whenever one was ever in question, he turned into Superman for a reason.

9. Fight for Inches

Baseball has long been known as a game of inches and it's imperative that we figure out ways to fight for every one of them. Base runners have a responsibility to maximize leads and secondaries. Runners must be in a position to dive to the back corner of the bag on pick-off attempts at first base and also must be prepared to quickly get back to the bag after their secondary lead when the ball is not put into play.

Reading the ball in the dirt and reading separation from the catcher are both critical in the fight for inches which quickly turn into ninety feet. It is also imperative that defenders are able to read swings and then position themselves appropriately. Every inch counts.

10. Apply Relentless Pressure

Get a lead, get a jump, go! From the creation of the *Let Them Play* organization, you would be hard-pressed to find another team at any level of baseball that has stolen more bases than we have swiped. Every kid has the green light, but this is given under the strict parameters that they must have an appropriate lead and an appropriate jump.

11. Statement Sprint

Run out to position between innings. Plain and simple, this sends a glorious message to the other team. The sprint does not have to be a hundred percent effort, but even taking the field at a ninety percent clip lets the other team know that we are fit for the battle.

Since the 1980s, Stanford has been one of the most successful college baseball programs. Growing up as a kid, I watched them win back-to-back national championships and the one thing I vividly remember about those teams is the full send effort in which they took the field. This is something that takes zero talent yet makes a huge statement and has the potential to return immense benefits.

12. Stay Ready to Be Ready

Master the pre-pitch routine . . . In the field or at bat, we must devise and then perfect a pre-pitch routine.

When I was in the field, I would flash the outs to the other outfielders; check the runners on base, and then pre-plan where I would go with the ball if it was hit directly at me, down the line, or in the gap. After the pitch, I would do a quick circle and arrive back at my exact position or make a slight adjustment based on the previous pitch. Before my at-bat, I would digest the situation, reaffirm my approach (line drive right-center field), and then do a quick stretch, tap my bat on my helmet, and get into the box.

Bench players must keep moving. A fun run to the foul pole between innings is a good way to stay hot and swinging off a tee, if available, will keep the bat-to-ball skills sharp and ready.

13. Prepare Endlessly

Everything we do should be done with this question in mind . . . "Does this make me a better baseball player?" Kobe Bryant was obsessed with basketball, and he talked about how he made the entire world his library. Everything he read, everything he watched, every conversation he had and just about everything he did was done under the pretense of making him a better basketball player. If we want to be great, we have no choice but to be obsessed and that obsession to be better at our craft goes far beyond the gym or playing field.

14. Respectfully Represent the Name on the Front of the Jersey

No obnoxious cursing, no bat slamming, no helmet tossing. Our attitude, effort, and language are a direct reflection of the team. We have had some incredibly talented kids play for us who never got a call back because of their obnoxious actions and behavior.

Bottom line . . . Don't be a Jackass.

15. No Sign Stealing

We are preparing the child for the road not the road for the child.

A couple of years ago, our *Let Them Play* team played against a top national team. The game was tight after the first couple of innings and then they busted it open and scored eight runs in one inning. After the sixth run crossed, we started paying attention to the verbiage and quickly realized the opposing coach was relaying the signs to the batter. Unfortunately, the damage was done. The next time we faced that same team, we devised a scheme to intentionally mix up the signs. The opposing team looked completely lost at the plate; we shut them out nearly the entire game and brought home an easy win. When we constantly pave the road for the kids, they will have no idea what to do when they inevitably hit the bumps.

16. No Stepping Out of the Batter's Box Unless after a Swing to Re-group

Barry Bonds was by far the greatest hitter I've ever seen in my lifetime and he never stepped out of the batter's box. If it worked for him, it should work for you. Baseball is a game that is meant to be played with tempo and somewhere along the way, the players abused the privilege of time and we are now dealing with a pitch clock at the highest level. Baseball is a very reactionary sport, therefore, the more time we have to think; the more likely our mind will get in the way and inhibit our well-trained natural reactions.

17. No Arguing with Umpires

That's what coaches are for. Umpires make mistakes and believe it or not, they are typically not trying to screw us.

Throughout the years of playing and coaching the game, I have encountered several situations where I knew in my heart that the umpire missed the call. Like most people, I get frustrated and emotionally charged each time, but the difference between when I was a young go-hard and now is that I have developed a process in dealing with horse-shit calls and that does not include emotionally arguing a call that the umpire will not change.

18. Fight for Outs

Hoard outs on defense and do not give them away on offense. Outs are the most valuable thing we possess. In a big league game, there are twenty-seven outs to give and get. In a high school game, there are twenty-one outs, and in a youth-level game, that number is reduced to eighteen (figuring there is no run-rule or time limit that gets imposed). That said, my experience in travel ball is that most games last just four innings before time expires or a run-rule comes into play; so in these cases, we are dealing with just twelve outs. Treat each one of them like the most precious resource imaginable, because they are.

19. Tempo Matters

Play fast, pitch quick, but don't hurry. The tempo of the game is typically dictated by the pitchers and how quickly they deliver the baseball. Slow pace inevitably prompted Major League Baseball to implement a pitch clock and although they are still sorting out some issues, thank goodness! Hitters, catchers, and coaches calling pitches can dictate the pace of the game as well. Be conscious of the pace, we must all do our part to be stewards of the game. As previously mentioned, a fast-paced game generally takes some of the unnecessary thinking out of the game and typically allows for your well-trained ability to work for you without letting the mind get in the way.

20. Play Free, Play Fearless

You Do You! Always fear the player who has nothing to lose. This is one of our main mottos with *Let Them Play*. When we can get the kids playing freely and fearlessly, we feel like we put them in the absolute best position to succeed. Pressure is one hundred percent self-imposed based on external circumstances and often our misguided interpretation of those circumstances. A popular acronym for F.E.A.R is "False Evidence Appearing Real" which turns out to be the ultimate inhibitor to progress and success.

21. Win the Pitch

The place is here, the time is now! In ultra-running, when faced with a very difficult task, I was taught to focus on putting one foot in front of the other. For instance, while running the Western States Hundred Miler, I hit a wall at mile eighty and felt like I couldn't go on. Instead of focusing on everything that was going wrong (fatigue, blisters on my feet, calorie deficiency), I decided to focus on the only thing that would actually propel me forward, taking one foot and putting it in front of the other one. Nothing else mattered.

In baseball, we can fall behind very easily, we could be playing a tight game or we can be beating the absolute bricks off teams. Regardless, our only focus should be on the immediate moment and our only goal should be to win the pitch . . . That's it.

22. Stay Juicy

Juicefull = Useful - Juiceless = F*ING Useless.

Energy (both positive and negative) is contagious and will infiltrate clubhouses and dugouts. On a scale of one to ten, we don't need players at a ten all of the time and obviously, we also don't want to ever see guys at a one. Work to stay consistently juicy at a seven, and always be sure to avoid the negative Neds doing their best to sink the ship. Energy creates energy and the very best teams and players we have had are able to positively feed off of one another's relentless positive vibes.

Twenty-Two Coaches Codes of Conduct

1. Let Them Play

Our job as coaches is to teach the kids how to autonomously play the game, not micromanage their every move. When we as coaches try to leave our footprint on the game, it not only slows the pace of play but also fails to teach the kids many of the basic needs and feels of the game.

For instance, we recently ran into a situation where one of our teams decided to wear wristbands full of signs. While on defense, the coach would call out numbers, and the shortstop, second baseman, pitcher, and catcher then would look down . . .

Here are a few observations:

1) This completely slowed the game down . . .

2) The aloof base runner they were trying to pick off started to pay extra attention.

3) The fielders became robotic and instead of naturally holding the runner, shit just got weird...

If we want to put on pick plays that actually will work, use verbal signals that will draw much less attention and allow the fielders to naturally move while not slowing the game down.

2. Situational Savagery

Outs and Outfielders-As soon as a runner gets on base, we will flash the outs to them until we get the outs flashed back to us. We then will have them check the defense to see where the other team is playing. Much like we discussed in the player code of conduct section, multiple signs take attention away from the game. This is the exact thing Ron Washington would have us do as our third base coach in Oakland, so if it was good enough to help us win twenty straight, I figure it is good enough for the kids.

3. Green Light Special

Every kid has the green light to steal unless the game situation dictates otherwise (down by several runs late in the game) or the privilege to run freely is abused. This will teach the players to test their limits and truly figure out what they are capable of from a lead and speed perspective. Ultimately, the kids don't like making outs any more than we like them making outs and they will eventually figure out how to get the best leads and jumps possible.

4. Maximize Inches

This is where our true coaching on the bases should be done. Teach kids how to maximize a base lead where they will be safe diving to the back corner of the bag. Shitty teams take shitty leads; great teams take great leads. Teach kids how to read slide steps and the difference between a leg kick, a slower slide step and a super quick one. From there, it's just a matter of them getting the proper lead, proper read, and proper jump.

5. Kiss-Keep it Simple Stupid!

Save the complex signs which unnecessarily slow the game down. Use flash signs and verbals. The verbiage we use is "On your own . . . Get a lead, get a jump, Go!" Flash signs could be outs given low instead of high or touching any part of the body, folding arms, etc. . . .

6. Forced Aggression-Must Steal

This will be a verbal or flash sign-Typically, this is three-one, two-two, or three-two counts. We love putting the runner in motion to avoid double play and love taking advantage of breaking ball counts. We tell all of our hitters to hit even if the base runner has a good jump. We don't want to waste a great pitch to hit just to advance the runner one base. If the hitter is able to get a ball into the outfield for a hit with the runner in motion, the moving runner is almost certainly going to end up on third base if not score.

7. Perfect Terminology

"Back on a line drive, back on a fly ball" until proper read by the runner is made with no outs. "Back on a line drive, halfway on a fly ball" with one out. "On contact" with two outs and "on the swing" with two outs and two strikes.

8. Swing Hard in Case You Hit It

No take sign-As mentioned before, if a player gets a great pitch to hit when a kid is stealing, we want them swinging. Think of every steal as a run and hit as opposed to a hit and run. Have base runners always peek in to find the ball. We also love swinging three-zero which is oftentimes the absolute best pitch to do damage on. Leading off an inning in a close game, I tell the boys, "Swing if you want, but it better be nuked." They end up taking ninety percent of the time, but if they have the balls to swing, let them.

9. Alertness Matters

Never take the eye of the ball! Never ever! Not the coach or the player. Always know where the ball is. It is incredible how many extra bases we will be able to take advantage of on late bobbles and drops. Also, bases are often left unoccupied with fielders paying no attention.

Make sure players are ready to run at any point and at any time. I used to rip third base all of the time when the third baseman would be playing way off the base and then turn his back to the infield between pitches.

10. Out Protection Police-No Sac Bunts

There are only eighteen outs to get and give in youth baseball; do not give a single one up. Bunts for base hits are fine; bunts to advance runners on bags we can steal anyway are not. Giving up outs in any fashion are big innings killers.

11. Players Play

Play your best defense to start the game and end with your best defense, but we highly encourage players to move positions on an inning-by-inning basis. We are here to develop "ball players" capable of playing all nine positions. That said, "any coach should have a feel of who the best defensive player or players are at each position." If we have two relatively equally talented third basemen but one is much better in the outfield, that kid goes to the outfield. It's not a bad idea to communicate that with the player as well as to why we make certain decisions.

12. Situational Sharing

Up eight runs or more, go for a "position buffet" where kids run out to the position of their choice. The only rule is it cannot be their usual position. The pitcher and catcher are excluded and still picked by the coach. Sure, we often end up with a 200-pound left-handed shortstop, but the experience and fun that the kids have with it far outweigh any sort of inconsequential play that may or may not be made.

13. Have a Plan but Stay Fluid

Unforeseen circumstances and game situations may dictate radical adjustments from the original plan. We recently had a pool play game that we felt we needed in order to get into the bracket. Realizing how good the other team was, at the last minute, we decided to go with one of our two aces. Ironically, he gave up six in the first inning, so plans changed again. We brought in one of our kids with lesser stuff but a great command to "put out the fire." After holding the other team in check, they eventually got to him forcing us to use our other ace to get the final out and hold onto a fifteen-thirteen win!

14. Correct, Do Not Condemn

Never pull a kid mid-inning because they made an error. Never verbally crush a kid on the field. Correct, but do not condemn. If the ultimate goal is to develop the kids, we must be proactive in preparation and less reactive in performance. Of course, I have felt like yanking kids off of the field mid-inning and to be honest, there have been scenarios where it probably would have been in the best interest of the team. That said, let's do our best to coach the kids up and let them know when they do things right as well as wrong.

15. Let Them Throw

Of course, you will have your dudes, but the goal should be to try to get everyone in to pitch in a weekend tourney. This keeps all kids fresh and we never know who we may have to call upon so getting even the non-pitchers experience on the mound is huge.

16. Endurance Is Earned

Unless it's the semi-final or championship game, a fifty-pitch count or three innings in one day is enough. Only go above the fifty number with kids that are trained to do so.

17. Long Toss Machines

All kids must play long toss every day of practice and games. This could be an entire book of its own but as an American culture, we throw way too little and pitch way too hard and way too often.

18. Call Less

Call pitches if you would like, but when we have a five-run lead or if for some reason we are getting crushed, let the kids call the game. It's incredible how much better the pace of play is without having to relay in the signs.

This also helps avoid sign stealing which has become all too common at just about every level from little league on up.

19. First Right of Refusal

Tell the pitcher he always has the right to shake off, just make sure they are ready to explain why. The last thing we want is a kid throwing a pitch if they do not believe in their ability to execute it.

20. Road Warriors

Always take visitors to all pool play games. This provides maximum at-bats. Almost in every game, we will have to pitch in the fourth so we might as well hit and put up runs. If we happen to lose, we don't have to pitch the fourth inning either which obviously saves arms.

21. Make Them Earn It

Shallow and aggressive on defense. If the other team gets hits, they are going to have to earn them. We have played a rover defense where we pull the CF in to about twenty feet beyond the second base bag as well as a five-man infield where the CF is completely in. In both cases, we pinch the outfield gaps with our left fielder and right fielder and shift according to the strength of our pitcher and batter tendencies.

22. Energy Bus Is Rolling and You Are the Driver

Kids feed off our energy. Bring the juice. Juicefull = Useful, Juiceless = Useless. How we talk, how we walk, how we carry ourselves as coaches is a reflection of the team as well as the organization. Like I tell the kids . . . Don't be a jackass!

Twenty-Two Parent Codes for Conduct

1. Get Kids to Practice and Games on Time

Just as the number one rule for the kids is to show up, it is the job of the parents to make sure they are there and on time.

2. Make Sure Kids Are Properly Equipped

I get it. The equipment these days can be expensive and plentiful. Find friends with kids who have played the sport, and there is a good chance that hand-me-downs will be available. "Play It Again" Sports is always a great option for valuable used equipment at cheap prices. As a parent, go over a uniform check from the ground up before leaving the house. Shoes, socks, sliding shorts, pants, belt, sleeves, jersey, batting gloves, hat, bat, and glove. Also, make sure your player has access to a water bottle as well as proper nutrition for fuel throughout the game.

3. Show Up

Come to as many games as possible—parents, family, and friends are the fan base and the kids (whether they say it or not) love the support.

4. Learn the Game

My mom bought the book "*Baseball for Dummies*" so she could better understand the game. My dad didn't know baseball very well at all, so instead of pretending to have all the answers, he simply asked a ton of questions. I couldn't have wished for more loving and supportive baseball parents.

5. Ask Questions

Mark Twain once said, "It's not what we don't know that hurts us but rather it's what we know for sure that just ain't so."

Even if we have a ton of experience in the game, it's imperative that we understand that the sport and techniques within the sport are constantly evolving. It's okay to have opinions but always remember to tactfully, and tastefully, give them with full understanding that there is a good chance that it will go in one ear and out the other.

A much better strategy is to consistently ask questions, listen, and then respond with encouragement that seems to fit both of your narratives. Let's remember that the most effective motivation is getting somebody to do what we want them to do because they want to do it!

6. Encourage Eternally

Sure, sometimes it's very difficult to encourage after your kid goes zero-four with four strikeouts or gives up nine runs without getting an out. That said, humor is one of the best ways to break the ice. At a recent Western Regional Ski Championship, my oldest daughter Chloe, aka Peanut, crashed in two of the races and missed a gate in the third so she had to hike back up the mountain to go around it. This obviously cost her several seconds, so in the one race she actually did finish, her result was the worst it's ever been. When she finally called after the most difficult three days of racing she has ever had, I answered the phone "Good job on the hike, honey." This immediately broke the ice and we had an amazing and ultra-productive conversation.

7. Let Coaches Coach

It sure is easy to coach from the stands, isn't it? For the most part, youth coaches are volunteers willing to spend their free time coaching our kids. Whether or not we agree with the decisions they may or may not make throughout the game is irrelevant to the fact that we should eternally be grateful for their service.

8. Never Condemn Your Kid or Other Players

Coach won't, you shouldn't. Do not condemn your kids, or anyone else's, before, during, or after a game.

9. 24-Hour Rule

Upset with your kid or coaches? Give it twenty-four hours to let emotions settle before having any sort of conversation. This generally will allow for a civilized, productive conversation as opposed to an emotionally charged irrational altercation that will never end well.

10. Support Extra Work

Hit three days a week. Take them to the gym. Pull up videos. Support the extra, outside of practice. This does not mean your kid needs his own personal hitting coach, but a tee and a net in the backyard are relatively cheap and easily accessible. Encourage your child to establish a routine and hold them accountable to stick to it.

11. Be the Gatekeeper of Fun

Continue to check in and remind kids that this is supposed to be fun :)

12. Deal with Your Kid as if He/She Is Somebody Else's

We are always harder on our kid so deal with him/her the same way you would deal with somebody else's.

This completely changes our tone of voice as well as the overall delivery while still making sure we hammer home the necessary information.

13. No Quitting

Start a season, and finish it.

14. Make Tools for Success Available

Twenty-two recommended books:

-*Wooden*

- *As A Man Thinketh*

-*Make Your Bed*

-*The Inner Game of Tennis*

-*The Mental Game of Baseball*

-*Heads Up Baseball*

-*Mental Toughness*

-*Mind Gym*

-*Flow*

-*The Secret*

-*The Power of Now*

-Chop Wood Carry Water

-Champion Minded

-Ego Is the Enemy

-Peak

-How Bad Do You Want It

-So Good They Can't Ignore You

-Tuesdays With Morey

-The Energy Bus

-Can't Hurt Me

-The F*IT List

-Daily Hustle 222

15. Do Not Negatively Address Other Team's Players, Coaches, Fans or Umpires

If it's that egregious, coaches will deal with the situation. Sure, your emotions will take over at some point, but it's up to you to bite your tongue and literally walk away!

16. Shhhh...

Other than nutrition, health concerns, or simple words of encouragement, do not talk to your kid during the game.

If this is an issue, once again, parents must remove themselves and watch from afar.

17. Be a Team

Show up and participate in as many team functions/get-togethers as possible. Each weekend we play, we typically have at least one team dinner or other activity where we invite the entire team. I am always quick to point out that if families cannot make it, it's okay. Yet, the bonding that typically takes place at these events is an integral part of team building so always make an effort to be there.

18. Swag Out

Wear the gear, support the squad! Our *Let Them Play* organization has some of the coolest gear imaginable and very few things are more satisfying than showing up at an event where we have multiple teams playing and seeing all the fluorescent orange and blue gear! When Colton got a chance to play for the USA 12U team in Aguascalientes, Mexico, the entire USA Baseball staff encouraged all family members to be "two feet in" by wearing red, white, and blue and cheering like the wild American savages we are.

19. Free and Fearless Parenting

We all want control, but it is imperative we let go and let the kids walk their own paths. We can help get them going in the right direction, but let's remember that oftentimes they will veer off the path and fall down several times before ultimately finding their way.

20. Out of View

Many kids have a tendency to look for their parents in the stands during the game for feedback between pitches or plays. If this is the case, parents are doing their kids a disservice by remaining in the line of sight. Part of letting them play is letting them handle their successes and failures on any given pitch. Out of sight typically means out of mind for the player, so on that note, go away :)

21. Do What You Can, with What You Have, Where You Are

Obviously, with eleven years of MLB experience, I help Colton however I can, but Tarah never played a day of baseball and has found ways to play catch, hit grounders, and throw BP! Our girls are competitive equestrians. Although I have been known to hop on a pony every now and again, I obviously don't have that experience. Get creative and experience the journey together. There is nothing more valuable in any relationship than shared experience.

22. Let Go

It's not up to us. Whether or not your kid plays in high school, college, or beyond is not going to be our decision, it will be one hundred percent up to them and the work they are willing to put in. At some point, they will be the ones who must become obsessed with their craft. There is no need to try to force anything; as the kids get older, the only thing parents will ever encounter is resistance and eventually rebellion. As a parent, we need to be supportive, but we are not responsible for the success or failure of our athletes' journey in sport, they are.

Conclusion

What are we hoping to get from all of this? Why do we invest our time, money, energy, and sometimes sanity, into youth sports? If it is simply to get Little Johnny to be the next Babe Ruth, we are missing a huge opportunity to develop Little Johnny into a full-spectrum savage instead of just one on the diamond.

Sports are unequivocally the single greatest tool for the multi-faceted experience a young child has. Competition, work ethic, goal setting, resilience, teamwork, forethought, grit, passion, grace, and empathy are all driving principles behind youth sports and should inevitably stick with the kids for the rest of their lives.

Let Them Play is a mantra that I first heard while watching the iconic 80s movie "Bad News Bears—Breaking Training," when Astros player Bob Watson started the chant that eventually gave the boys a chance to keep playing. Since then, for me personally, "*Let Them Play*" developed into a mentality, a way of life, and eventually an organization aimed at helping young men and women reach their maximum potential. Yet, just like any other words spoken in life, without specific direction and specific action taken, they are just words and don't mean a damn thing.

The above *Let Them Play* creed and codes of conduct are by no means set in stone, and as we travel this road together, let's remember to be fluid, growing with our experience. It has only been through my extensive successes and failures as a player, coach and parent that I was able to gather the invaluable knowledge that gave me the confidence and passion to both write and share this book.

The great thing about gathering experiences is that we are able to learn from what has worked and what has not and then it's up to us to make the appropriate and necessary adjustments. Regardless of where you are in your playing, coaching, or parenting journey, it is with great hope that the *Let Them Play* guide will be able to serve as a beautiful guiding light through the arduous journey of both sports and life.

With passion, energy, and effort, LFG!